HISTORY EXPLORERS

NATIVE AMERICANS

by Evelyn Wolfson

Consultant: Dr. Peter Whiteley

Curator of North American Ethnology, American Museum of Natural History

This book looks at the lives and traditions of four tribes:
the Iroquois, Cherokee, Sioux, and Hopi.

D1088848

ticktock

North American edition copyright © *ticktock* Entertainment Ltd. 2010
First published in North America in 2010 by *ticktock* Media Ltd.,
The Old Sawmill, 103 Goods Station Road, Tunbridge Wells, Kent TN1 2DP, U.K.

ISBN 978-1-84696-214-1
Tracking number: 3231LPP0909
Printed in China
9 8 7 6 5 4 3 2 1

Picture credits (t=top; b=bottom; c=center; l=left; r=right; OFC=outside front cover; OBC=outside back cover): Alamy: 11l, 17cr, OBCb.
Courtesy of the Division of Anthropology, American Museum of Natural History: 9tr (artifact catalog number 50/6525AB), 9cr (50/6492),
9br (1/4965), 11br (10/24), 13tr (50/7267), 13cr (50/7268), 13br (501/5622), 17br (50/4362), 23cr (50/9404). British Museum: 10.
Corbis: OFC, 2–3, 4bl, 5, 6–7, 8, 12, 13l, 15r, 16, 18, 19, 21, 22, 23l, 23br. G. Peter Jemison: 11tr. North Wind Picture Archives: 9tl.
Susanne Page: 20–21 (main). Smithsonian Institution: 17l. Woolaroc Museum, Bartlesville, Oklahoma: 14–15.

Every effort has been made to trace the copyright holders, and we apologize in advance for any unintentional omissions.
We would be pleased to insert the appropriate acknowledgment in any subsequent edition of this publication.

Contents

Glossary

On the last page, there is a glossary
of words and terms.
The glossary words appear
in **bold** in the text.

Spreading across the land

The first Americans came from Asia and settled in North America between 60,000 and 12,000 years ago.

These peoples spread across North America in small groups. Some settled in the forests of the northeast and others in the far north, where it is cold.

Some peoples chose to live in the southeast, where it is warm all year long. Others settled in the hot deserts of the southwest.

This Sioux man is wearing a traditional headdress.

Because each **environment** was different, the people developed their own ways of finding food, building houses, making clothes, and giving thanks to the **spirits**.

ARCTIC

BLACKFOOT

SUBARCTIC

NORTHWEST COAST

HAIDA

KWAKIUTL

PLATEAU

FLATHEAD
NEZ PERCE

CALIFORNIA

SHOSHONE

POMO

GREAT BASIN

YOKUTS

CHUMASH

NAVAJO   PUEBLO
HOPI   APACHE

SOUTHWEST

Over thousands of years, the people became hundreds of different Native American nations, each with their own **culture**.

The first Americans

MAP OF NORTH AMERICA

INUIT

SIOUX

CREE

ALGONQUIN

IROQUOIS

SHAWNEE

GREAT PLAINS

NORTHEAST

CHEROKEE

SOUTHEAST

CHOCTAW

SEMINOLE

PAWNEE

This map shows the homelands of some of the Native American nations and the different environments of North America.

As they traveled across the land, native peoples made drawings on rocks and in caves. These drawings are called PETROGLYPHS.

The EAGLE is a symbol of strength and courage to many Native Americans.

Important lessons

Long ago, Native Americans did not have a written language. It was very important to LISTEN AND REMEMBER. Children didn't go to school but instead learned by watching and copying grownups.

Children learned **origin stories** and **legends** from listening to **storytellers**. Each part of the country had its own special stories.

A ceremonial dance at a powwow

Boys began to hunt and fish with the men when they were ten years old. Some boys learned how to grow corn and other crops.

Girls helped the women. They cared for their younger brothers and sisters and collected moss and furry seed heads as diaper material to put inside babies' **cradleboards**.

A Navajo woman with a baby in a cradleboard

Different cultures

Headdresses were worn by GREAT PLAINS warriors. Each feather represented a brave deed.

Children still learn tribal **traditions** from grownups today. This picture shows families at a powwow. These gatherings of many different tribes are held every year.

Tribes of the northwest coast carved stories on wooden TOTEM POLES.

People of the longhouse

Tribes of the Iroquois settled in the forests of the northeast. These tribes included the Mohawk, Oneida, Onondaga, Cayuga, Seneca, and Tuscarora.

The Iroquois lived in wooden longhouses, made from frames of young trees covered with elm bark.

An Iroquois man stands alongside the reconstruction of a longhouse.

Each longhouse was home to ten or more families from the same family group, or clan. *Bear*, *Turtle*, *Beaver*, and *Deer* are some Iroquois clan names.

8

Inside a longhouse, fires for cooking and heating divided the families' living space. Above each fire was a smoke hole in the roof.

This woodcut picture shows Iroquois families harvesting corn.

The Iroquois planted large gardens of corn, beans, and squashes. The beans climbed up the corn stalks, and squashes grew around the bottom. This arrangement was called the "three sisters."

Iroquois artifacts

MUSIC was made using drums and rattles.

This Iroquois RATTLE is made from a turtle shell filled with pebbles.

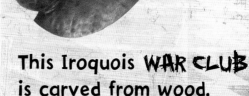

This Iroquois WAR CLUB is carved from wood.

The Iroquois Confederacy

The Iroquois tribes had a long history of fighting with one another. Around 1,000 years ago, five Iroquois tribes formed a special group called THE IROQUOIS CONFEDERACY.

The Mohawk, Oneida, Onondaga, Cayuga, and Seneca tribes agreed to live in peace under one imaginary longhouse that stretched across their **territory**. Later, the Tuscarora joined the Confederacy.

Wampum belts were made from strings of shell beads.

This is a wampum belt. The designs of wampum belts recorded important agreements and events.

Today, the Confederacy chiefs still meet to make laws and decide on **customs**.

Mohawk children at a powwow

Iroquois tribes still get together at powwows and festivals. These Mohawk children are taking part in a **smoke dance** competition.

Iroquois culture

The Iroquois believe that life began when Sky Woman fell from the sky.

Sky Woman landed on a turtle's back, which grew to become TURTLE ISLAND, the Iroquois name for North America.

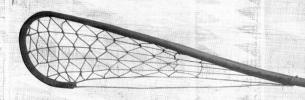

LACROSSE is the best-known Iroquois game. Players throw a ball and use a net attached to a stick to catch it. Sometimes tribes played lacrosse instead of going to war!

Villagers of the southeast

The Cherokee were SKILLED FARMERS who grew crops in the rich, dark soil of the southeast. They settled in small villages along rivers and streams.

Cherokee families often had two houses—a rectangular house made from wood and grass for the summer and a cone-shaped winter house covered with clay or woven mats for warmth.

Summer house

Winter house

A reconstruction of traditional Cherokee houses

Cherokee women worked in the fields and made clothes from deerskin. Cherokee men hunted for deer and bears with bows and arrows.

The Cherokee grew corn, beans, squashes, and tobacco. Corn could not be eaten until the yearly Green Corn Ceremony. This great festival was celebrated in the fall after the last crop had ripened.

A Cherokee man wears traditional clothing during a ceremonial dance.

Cherokee artifacts

During the GREEN CORN CEREMONY, men danced and shook rattles made from **gourds** to thank the spirits for a bountiful harvest.

Tribal leaders smoked tobacco in CLAY PIPES during important ceremonial events.

This emerald AMULET, or lucky charm, was worn by a Cherokee chief.

The Trail of Tears

In the early 1800s, **non-Indian settlers** began to want the Cherokee's farmland for themselves. In 1838, the **U.S. government** made 15,000 Cherokee give up their land and leave their homes.

The Cherokee people were forced to march west to what was called **Indian Territory.** During the trip, they were guarded by U.S. soldiers and Native Americans who were working for the U.S. government.

Thousands of Cherokee died of disease and starvation on the long march. The journey is known as the "Trail of Tears."

This painting by Robert Lindneux is called **The Trail of Tears.**

Some Cherokee refused to leave. They hid in the mountains.

Cherokee history

A Cherokee man named SEQUOYA made up an alphabet so that his people could write down their spoken language.

The alphabet turned all the different Cherokee sounds into only 85 characters.

In 1828, the Cherokee published the first Native American newspaper, the CHEROKEE PHOENIx.

Buffalo hunters

A sea of grass grew on North America's Great Plains. Many grazing animals fed on the grass, especially BUFFALO. To the Sioux, the buffalo was the most honored and respected of all the creatures on the plains.

American buffalo

Every year, large herds of buffalo **migrated** across the plains.

16

The Sioux relied on the buffalo for food and for **hides** to make clothes and tepees. So when the buffalo moved, the Sioux followed.

This painting shows Sioux hunters chasing buffalo.

Sioux horses could outrun buffalo. They were trained to run close alongside the mighty animals so that the hunters could shoot arrows or throw spears into the buffalo's necks.

Hunters and warriors

Great Plains Indians performed ceremonies and **rituals** before and after buffalo hunts.

APPALOOSAS are horses with a short, fast stride. They are bred by the Sioux.

Warriors held their HIDE SHIELDS in one hand when on horseback. The shields protected them against enemy arrows.

Life on the plains

The Sioux lived in CONE-SHAPED TENTS called tepees. These portable houses were just right for their **nomadic** lifestyle. Tepees were covered with buffalo hides and had frames made from large wooden poles.

A Sioux dancer in ceremonial clothes stands beside a tepee.

Buffalo herds moved quickly, and Sioux families had to be ready to follow. Women could take down a tepee in only 15 minutes.

When moving from place to place, Sioux men made a travois, or carrier, by attaching the narrow ends of tepee poles to the back of a horse.

This photograph shows Sioux children riding on a travois.

Entire villages moved several times during a single season of buffalo hunting. When making camp, Sioux families arranged their tepees in a circle.

This painting shows Sioux families in a tepee village.

Sioux artifacts

During battle, Sioux warriors would try to get close enough to touch an enemy but not kill him. This was called COUNTING COUP.

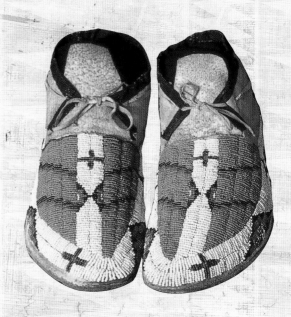

Warriors used coup sticks to touch their enemies.

These Sioux MOCCASINS are made from buffalo hide. They are decorated with porcupine quills.

19

People of the mesas

The Hopi have lived in the deserts of the southwest for THOUSANDS of years. Today, Hopi people still live in northern Arizona. They live on top of three flat tabletop hills with steep sides. These hills are called mesas.

This picture shows the Hopi mesa village of Walpi.

One mesa village, Oraibi, is 1,000 years old. In ancient times, the mesas served as natural protection against enemy attacks.

Hopi houses are made out of sandstone and adobe, a sun-dried clay.

Hopi houses are built on top of one another.

The houses are stacked, with the roof of one house serving as a terrace for the house above. Ladders make it easy to climb from house to house.

Hopi myths and legends

These stone drawings show **TAWA**, the sun god, and **SPIDER WOMAN**.

In the beginning of time, they sang a magic song and formed animals, birds, and insects. Then they shaped men and women and placed them all on Earth.

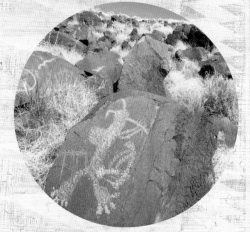

This stone drawing shows **KOKOPELI**, a mythical humpbacked flute player. Kokopeli plays and dances when people are sad.

Desert farmers

Corn has been important to Hopi life for thousands of years. It grows well in the **HOT DESERT CLIMATE**. Hopi men also grow gardens of beans, squashes, and pumpkins.

This Hopi farmer is growing corn in the dry desert.

To grow crops, you need rain. The kachinas are spirits who help make it rain.

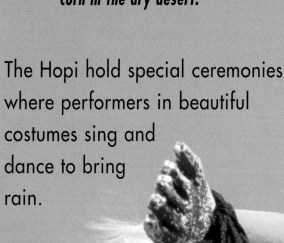

The Hopi hold special ceremonies where performers in beautiful costumes sing and dance to bring rain.

At some ceremonies, dancers perform as kachina spirits who call out to the clouds over the fields of corn. Some ceremonies include dancing with live rattlesnakes.

This is a wooden kachina doll.

Hopi artists carve wooden kachina dolls. They are given to Hopi girls at kachina ceremonies.

Hopi life and customs

Corn roots can reach 20 ft. (6m) underground, helping the plant find water in the dry sand.

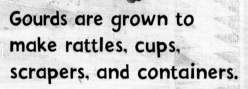

Gourds are grown to make rattles, cups, scrapers, and containers.

Young Hopi women wore their hair in two rolls, called BUTTERFLY WHORLS, until they got married.

23

Glossary

CRADLEBOARDS Flat pieces of wood used for carrying babies. A mother carries a cradleboard on her back.

CULTURE The way of life and beliefs of a group of people.

CUSTOMS Things that are done in a particular way again and again. They are handed down from one generation to the next.

ENVIRONMENT The place where a person lives and the things that affect that place such as the weather and type of land.

GOURDS Hard-skinned vegetables that are related to pumpkins.

HIDES Animal skins.

INDIAN TERRITORY The part of North America that is now Oklahoma.

LEGENDS Tales about supernatural creatures or events.

MIGRATED Moved from one area to another. Animals migrate to a new place to find more food or to breed.

NOMADIC Describes people who move from place to place along with their homes.

NON-INDIAN SETTLERS Settlers who came from Europe and claimed for themselves the lands where Native Americans had lived for thousands of years.

ORIGIN STORIES Tales that explain how a group of people came to be.

RITUALS Religious or important ceremonies where certain actions are carried out in a set order.

SMOKE DANCE A dance said to imitate the way in which people fanned smoke from longhouse fires—out through the holes in the roof.

SPIRITS Unexplained forces in nature, like those that control the weather; lifelike forces within living things.

STORYTELLERS People who tell stories that keep tribal traditions alive. They teach the history of the land and show the proper way for humans to live together.

TERRITORY The Iroquois area across the upper part of New York.

TRADITIONS Beliefs, actions, or ways of doing things that are handed down from one generation to the next.

U.S. GOVERNMENT Within 100 years of arriving in North America, the non-Indian settlers organized themselves into colonies. In 1776, the settlers formed the government of the United States. The new government made laws that the Native Americans had to live by.

Index